The Domesticity of Giraffes

Judith Beveridge

The Domesticity of Giraffes

PICARO PRESS

For Chris

The author gratefully acknowledges that this project was assisted by the Australian Government through the Australia Council, its arts funding and advisory body.

The Domesticity of Giraffes
ISBN 978 1 920957 44 5
Copyright © Judith Beveridge 1987
Cover: Giraffe by Keith Roper (1913)
https://www.flickr.com/photos/keithroper/11392360793/
(http://creativecommons.org/licenses/by/2.0/)
PhotosForClass.com

First published 1987 by Black Lightning Press

This edition published 2017 by
Picaro Press – an imprint of
GINNINDERRA PRESS
PO Box 3461 Port Adelaide 5015 Australia
www.ginninderrapress.com.au

Contents

The Domesticity of Giraffes	7
Flamingo Park	9
For Rilke	10
Making Perfume	12
Girl Swinging	14
Catching Webs	16
Orb Spider	18
Fox in a Tree Stump	20
The Lyre Birds	22
Marsupial	24
The Caterpillars	26
Monarch Butterflies	28
Ladybirds	29
Child Fishing	30
Mulla Bulla Beach	34
The Fishermen	35
Reels	37
Mud Crabs, Low Tide	40
Eyepiece	42
Japanese Cranes	44
At the End of the Day	46
Situation	47
Last Walk	48
On Polling Day	50
The Bee Keeper	52
White Peacock	54
The Herons	56
In the Park	57
Walking in the Angophora Forest at Night	58
Streets of Chippendale	60

Wind	62
The Two Brothers	64
Dining Out	66
Flower of Flowers	67
Chinese Explorer in Africa: 15th Century	68
Hannibal on the Alps	69
The Eunuch's Lament	70
The Blue Bulb	72
Address from the Curved City	73
The Dispossessed Angels	74
Angel-glass	76
The Clerical Angel	78
Performing Angels	81
The Fall of Angels	83
Mirrors	85
My Name	86
The Workday	87
The Book of Birds	88
Invitation	90

The Domesticity of Giraffes

She languorously swings her tongue
like a black leather strap as she chews
and endlessly licks the wire for salt
blown in from the harbour.
Bruised-apple eyed she ruminates
towards the tall buildings
she mistakes for a herd:
her gaze has the loneliness of smoke.

I think of her graceful on her plain –
one long-legged mile after another.
I see her head framed in a leafy bonnet
or balloon-bobbing in trees.
Her hide's a paved garden of orange
against wild bush. In the distance, running
she could be a big slim bird just before flight.

Here, a wire-cripple –
legs stark as telegraph poles
miles from anywhere.
She circles the pen, licks the wire,
mimics a gum-chewing audience
in the stained underwear of her hide.
This shy Miss Marigold rolls out her tongue

like the neck of a dying bird.
I offer her the fresh salt of my hand
and her tongue rolls over it
in sensual agony, as it must
over the wire, hour after bitter hour.
Now, the bull indolently
lets down his penis like a pink gladiolus
drenching the concrete.

She thrusts her tongue under his rich stream
to get moisture for her thousandth chew.

Flamingo Park

They step out on the long stems
of their legs, stand before mirrors
placed by their keepers. Intoxicated
like actresses, they enter as through
the foyer of Le Grand Hôtel.
See their many faces under stars
like beauty-contest lights.
These mirrors are swelling their numbers
to breeding size. Their simple pond
has now swollen to a glass resort.
These birds of rich feathers
have views to trees and water and walk
at every turn into Property, becoming
the Palace Birds who lift or leisurely tuck back
the long silk scarves of their necks.
This is the Royal Garden where summer
has a pink musk centre. Next door,
the cassowaries (wearing stone-age axes
on their heads) and crop-haired emus
protest, stomp their pens, squawk like pickets.
But the flamingoes – those pink
Entrants with Revlon cheeks – see the trick.
They have fooled their keepers (entrepreneurs
eyeing the mirrors like turnstiles)
and will not breed. They just peer
into the long dining hall
of perfectly reproducing mirrors,
lift heads like cocktail glasses, stride
into their most exclusive Club.

For Rilke

You can cup your ear in your hand
and hear your voice turn all light and clear
in its depths –
but we hear nothing, just the noisy world.

And the world loves to be noisy.
It loves to make a clatter,
to play itself with our tongues,
its diamond styluses,
loudly
and for long periods.

But you are your own quiet singing.
The world sets speakers above our heads
(even when we sleep)
blaring at tremendous decibels –
and we can't hold out against it,
in the morning
the words of its song
pummel our lips awake.

Our hearts – they're like utensils
taken from their original uses
and put into the world's jug band.
Listen to us: we are like bottles
filled to different levels and then struck
for our various resonances:

not like you, poet –
your voice pure as a tuning fork
independent
of what it's struck off; the gentle
absolute humming of steel
against which we are, to ourselves,
severe grating, unbearable
dissonance.

Making Perfume

So, that summer I picked everything:
the hibiscus that shut at six o'clock,
the white-pollened flower
I called The Baker's Daughter,
the yellow rose that lasted weeks beyond its season
and the great pale flower with the cold look –
Queen in the Tower.

Then I took some bottles from their cupboards
and their lids twirled off and their perfume
came three voices high in my head.
I lined them like wineglasses on the sill
and filled each with petals and water
and gave them keyboard names like
Chandelier and Tier on Golden Tier.

I remember how I lived that summer
in a room with a thousand windows in blue and green.
I'd stay out late to pick and soak the petals
and pour them into bottles and bury them in the earth
with a made-up name for a simple flower plus water.
Later, I'd wash and line the bottles on the sill
and read their labels until each one rang

a terrace of bells in my head.
I mourned the bottles I named for my heroines of hopeless love
and stood them in kitchen tap water
and stored them out of the light.
I dreamt of Balls, dinner roses,
a woman gently naming herself to herself.

Now, I wonder whatever happened to Lavinia,
the Fourteen Nights, Ballet Blanc,
the fragrance in the blue twirled bottle
I named Pirouette.
Months later I probably poured them down the sink.

But no-one suspected that summer
why my eyes were suddenly circled with a dark pencil,
why my cheeks had the faint glow of day,
why I swished my skirts as I moved.

I kept the bottles with me, moved them about the room
vowed not to open them for seven years,
and named them after the girl kept at home
who never stopped saying as she stirred her pots:
'Oh, I wish, I wish, I wish…'

Girl Swinging

A swing grinds on its chains.
A child sits pushing.
There's no eucalyptus,
atlas pine, or flowering ash,

no other child is calling
from the tender modulations of leaves:
just each note
of her ringing heart,
the feeling of being pushed
into the air.

I often think about
the long process that loves
the sound we make.
It swings us until
we've got it by heart:
the music we are.
But sometimes I sense

the child's life
twisted away from its
own mystery: the voice
struck, held back.

I long to be a symphony
levitated by grace notes.

Quietly, I wait,
listening to myself
when, suddenly innocent of misery –
that feeling comes
of being lifted into the air:

that clear singing
above bare stones, above
the common rattle
of chains.

Catching Webs

A fragrance would call me out of the house:
threads sweet with pollens.

I'd walk into any alien zone or quiet radar –
(those stolen threads always fitted so close).
And sometimes coming back into the house
I'd feel a thread break across my lips.

I remember the white purdah of those days
spent amongst the undergarments of trees,
air crisp as dressmaker's paper
against the bright textile of summer.

I was a child with so much of my world
snatched up in a mending, as life unspooled
from my fingers though I could not feel
those long strands training to the South.

I'd go out after meals to watch a thread
trace itself on the sky and wait for it
to drift into my hands; or walk amongst
the flowers draped in the negligée

of their leaves. I remember sky
on rising sky, cool air on my lips,
stars that sewed themselves onto the air
like buttons in order of brightness

and a child's heart pushing in
like a needle, making a pattern
of its incisions; making a web
out of the stitch of its own silence:

thin thin darning that holds the heart separate
from its white dress. I knew a thread
could be pulled right through
the human body. In the fragrant air,

I felt the moon in my blood, trailing its wedding.

Orb Spider

I saw her, pegging out her web
thin as a pressed flower in the bleaching light.
From the bushes a few small insects
clicked like opening seed-pods. I knew some
would be trussed up by her and gone next morning.
She was so beautiful spinning her web
above the marigolds the sun had made
more apricot, more amber; any bee
lost from its solar flight could be gathered
back to the anther, and threaded onto the flower
like a jewel.
        She hung in the shadows
as the sun burnt low on the horizon
mirrored by the round garden bed. Small petals
moved as one flame, as one perfectly-lit hoop.
I watched her work, produce her known world,
a pattern, her way to traverse
a little portion of the sky;
a simple cosmography, a web drawn
by the smallest nib. And out of my own world
mapped from smallness, the source
of sorrow pricked, I could see
immovable stars.

    Each night
I saw the same dance in the sky,
the pattern like a matchbox puzzle,
tiny balls stuck in a grid until shaken
so much, all the orbits were in place.
Above the bright marigolds
of that quick year, the hour-long day,
she taught me to love the smallest transit,
that the coldest star has a planetesimal beauty.
I watched her above the low flowers
tracing her world, making it one perfect drawing.

Fox in a Tree Stump

I gripped the branch
and waited in a paddock that ran on
over harder and harder earth.
Leaving me with smoke and the stick
to beat the fox, my uncle drove off.

Terror barrel-rode through my stomach.
I knew my uncle's quick rabbit-skinning hands,
his arms like dry river beds dammed at the shoulders,
his voice harsh, kelpie-cursing
would not understand if I let the fox run to the bush.

Fox-hairs of dust sweated my palms.
I stood in the exhaust of leaves
the short time it takes a tongue
to teach into a hurting body and strike ashes.

A twig snapped. The fox stood, coughing.
The branch on its neck
rang like a shot:
a shot so loud it shook out a flock
of galahs from their trees,
cracked like a wave
the buried sleep of rabbits.

When my uncle came back, he threw
the charred body into a ditch.
I turned away kicking earth over the blood spots of fire
and prayed not to waken
another animal from the wheat.
I was nine years old. All my life
I'd stuck close to my yelled name.

I was a child praying for the dark
each time the sun caught my uncle's eye.

The Lyre Birds

Somewhere in the bush, hiding as long as they can,
domestic as soil, they scrape the hard earth
with their feet, making serious men-at-work sounds –
or pretending in their voices to be other than themselves.

These birds, from old-country Australia,
when everything was bush-fire charcoal, scrub.
Shy of their own language,
they exist still in their wingless rituals

amongst the bush vowels of the parrots,
the mynas, the Dubbo-voiced galahs.
They can imitate any sky, any tree, bird by bird; make
a branch crack with fire in a whipbird's throat.

Not much to see: tail like brown bracken and built
for miles and miles of the same scrub.
You can hear them call to each other
with a whole country's voice: pine-high whispers,

water falling, a magpie's swagman whistle,
the downpour of wings, twitterings
from the long coops of grasses and they can steal
the wind's voice: a stock whip at their throats; or repeat

note by industrial note the timber-mills, chain-saws...
But I imagine them long ago, when all was bush –
at dusk, wandering in pairs –
relaxed peacocks among the old gums;

they believed they were the feathered men
who danced the corroborees.
Now, scavengers of sound, like migrants
they've learned to live off foreign sounds in a new country,

to repeat another country's parrot culture,
to keep anonymous, alive.
But sometimes they forget and call to each other
in their own tongue, remembering a time

when ring after ring of men stopped,
got up, stomped the ground, danced, stomped again,
danced and sang their own voices back to them.

Marsupial

I am happy to live with them, though they pre-date us;
the ones with bruised eyes and an outback look,
in their fur, grey dust and red rock,
in their teeth the stains of grasses,
in their stride the long legs of miles –
and to see in their barely weathered skulls, their ancestors
who crouched on the plains at dusk.

But sometimes looking at them, there is a feature
not accountable to time or habitat: a vague link
to a lost continent.
This country of old holes, graves, tree-stumps,
of tribal animals double-mothering their young;
seed-gatherers of equal work, free but naturally domestic,

not bond servants to the taste of blood or work of seasons;
of creatures who live their simple culture in a soil
that can shut down for summers against the simplest root.
Beside them, I feel like a new animal unlicked at birth,
scratching for fosterage in a place
transplanted like topsoil from Europe full
of service animals. Ground can shift

and leave species to start up again.
But the earth evolves its creatures: whatever
its conditions we adapt, match our landscapes.
So I see them, sleepy and relaxed
in the eucalyptus dens of our continent,
or wandering the yellow bush at evening,

carrying young in the warm swags of their wombs,
loving the land; itinerant, but placed.
I envy them their hippie lives, these marsupials,
the alternative animals, doped on leaves,
happy to retire on the oldest landmass.
This queer evolution won, the long arbitration
with Nature in the courts of Gondwanaland.

The Caterpillars

On the headland to the lighthouse,
a brown detour of caterpillars
crimped end-to-end across the road.

Poke away the pilot and the line
would break up, rioting,
fingering for the scent.
Put him back, they'd straighten.
You could imagine them humming
their queue numbers.

I've only seen such blind following
in the patient, dull dole queues,
or old photos of the Doukhobors,
the world's first march of naked people.

I watched over the line for hours
warding off birds whose wings, getting close,
were like the beating of spoons
in deep bowls. I put a finger to the ground
and soft prickles pushed over,
a warm chain of hair.

This strange sect, wrapped in the sun
like their one benefit blanket
marched in brotherhood and exile.

Later, a group of boys
(their junta minds set on torture)
picked off the leader.
Each creature contorted,
shut into its tight burr.
I could only stand like a quiet picket
and watch the rough panic.

I remember them, those caterpillars,
pacifists following their vegetable passion –
lying down in the road and dying
when they could no longer touch each other.

Monarch Butterflies

for Yvette Christianse

I love the way they open into two broad wings,
trembling like paper and so thin –
you'd think they could only live wrapped up.
But for the brief time they are open
and given to sunlight, they make their way
drifting with the wind – a litter
above traffic, above newsstands.
But where do they go, yellow with pollen
the way our hands are black?
They travel at night over water
by resting on anything floating
and carry their wings into the open boulevards.
You'd think they could be stopped
by any breeze stronger than a child's breath;
or that a million years might pass
before they lift out of trees
like leaves turning red and weightless.
These bright lapels that are so briefly
matched to the flowers, they hover
for the sweet sharp scent; and tremble
as they place along tip ends
a weightless eyelash. They mate
and close their wings privately a moment
like letters. Passing from one place
to the next they nod and lift into headwinds
to cross over borders. You'd believe
they're the airborne consorts of only
saintly souls, of the just and merciful sovereigns.
They fly, they alight one on top
of the other, they hang in high chains –
they arrive like streamers.

Ladybirds

In the body of the night sky, their slow
progression. On chrysanthemums, on cabbages,
the fallow rose, the potato vine –
their constellations stud each leaf.

You could pick them, but they'd die
in your hand. They climb the brick path,
tilt a grey-green leaf. I see
their black and cumquat spots

when the insects like machines
are digging the earth. They're
like glass eyes in soft faces of dolls
we loved as children, much slept with.

Now they rise as tiny sparks,
fire chips lifting higher than all
the safaris of ash. I call them
Easter beetles for their silent

ascension, for their colour,
for their stillness in the hand,
unlike other wings skirreting
like militant angels. They are lost

on marigolds, in a night sky's
scattered brilliance. I think of
some lost remembered face
with a simple name and a pale peace.

Child Fishing

I.

He holds a green nylon line around a cork core:
The weight of the apple he half eats.
Beside him, his father's reel races like a stopwatch,
clicks over, turns silent in the sea's lining of lead.
He casts into the spray, the driftwood.
Weed searches the ocean for its lost grip.

He hears his father curse the fish.
The rod almost doubles over, the sea
moans in its shells, its spiralled headphones
and the beach fills with the frenzy
of the winding reel. Along the clean gashes of gills
fish are lifted into names and gravity. A boy, he wanted

them loose and light as the moving, sinking kites
he casually held a string to. But his father
pulls them in, stiff as trophies, pulling at
the barbed clefs in their mouths, and in a sleet
of fish scales cleans them, unstitching their intestines
with an intricate haberdashery of hooks.

II.

In the wind a few scales carry. The boy catches
their scattered jewels. But the necessary gadgets
give death a stainless setting. Will his father
pass him the pocket knife, will his hands feel colder
than the threadbare weather when he incises
the fishes' gills and their greasy, satinette skins?

Lost green weed surges through the waves
as his father casts in. Sinkers
are like birthstones for the dead.
He wants to go home. It is dark. He watches the sea
glide under a polished deck of moonlight, the tide fill out
with light and a wave turn along precise pleats.

III.

He feels something sinking into his life;
feels a storm's ready-sinkered lines;
feels his voice wasting in air like a gill.
In water, he sees himself as the discarded snarl
languishing towards the surface.
His line quakes like a handrail. He waits

for the first sounds on the surface
but hears only the reel ticking.
He dreams of the voice of his father
like a soft towel patted on his shivering skin.
But he hears him cursing the fish, saying names
on his rosary of hook and gut, scraping the knife.

IV.

Against a dark sea, he knows he can be taken
by a single cord and let drift. He knows no reel
stops at the shore. He looks at his father –
a weight he no longer feels buoyed to.
Weightless against a dark sea, he wonders when
he will be taken by a single cord and let drift.

V.

He would like to thread scales onto a hook and slide
them up into his line, like a trinket,
to colour them like sequins, a craft of buttons,
a charm against the reel's anti-chanting
and to wait for a tug on his line
to unravel him from the shore, past cuttlebone

dumped like sea plaster, past driftwood
and the weed washed up, to lift him into the white
rubble of spray and out to depths hitched under coral.
A dream his father would curse him for
as he stands with the half-bitten apple in his hands
and the lines are heavy, toyless kites

in a sunken sky that can jewel the light,
make a boy afraid. He knows the reel
can pulverise his jewels to grit as he stares
at the beach, the ground lockets of shells
that once held his portrait. He knows
he can no longer be buoyed to his innocence,

to the bell of his heart against danger.
He knows his father will hand him the trophy
of the knife and the reel to be worn at the wrist:
an amulet with which to blaspheme at the tides.
He knows he will let the souls of fish
fly from their gills, that he will scrape the knife

along the shields of their sides and his father
will look towards the sea with a blessing.

Mulla Bulla Beach

Before the sea stops a long mile out
I hear the blades of fishermen scotching the rocks

and their reels beginning to grind like bicycle gears.
The sand is smooth but for weed,

jellyfish clear as surgical gloves.
I watch the men who fish all day, eyes fast

on the water, who were born hearing the sea always there.
A place will seep into the voice

of any local. I walk where sponges grow
like moist yeast, a new world to me,

but familiar. I squeeze the sea out.
Part of that plain voice goes dead.

It is the talk of people living here all year round
who wish just to be left alone.

Now, at almost dark, a dead confetti
of fish scales sticks to the rocks.

There's no word but the sea's and tide-winded shells
pacing quietly as shore-runners:

though sometimes, there is a line, a murmur
winding and unwinding in the shells.

The Fishermen

The air's a torn weave
of sea-spray,
the wind lifts my blouse
a little from my shoulders.
I see birds thin as apple cores,
the sun eating what life
there is. I listen:

the wind and the sea
move the same sound through broken shells.
And sometimes that sound
will never leave your hands;
it will trail like something
caught on the tips
of your fingers.

All night, all you can see
are the faint white casts
of the fishermen
and a shore that seems
to be drifting.
I cup my hands,
hear my blood in shells

dead voices spill into.
The fishermen stand
with one artery open
to the sea. The moon glows
in their breath
starched by the cold
and white water flares up.

I hear the gasp in the shells
when the shore drifts.
I stand right at the edge
with the men,
but at a distance
and threads pump back
a secret voice

into my open hands.
We don't call, the one
tense strand is enough.
All night, our white breath
crosses into the cold
ouija-world of the sea.

Reels

This one is fast, infinitely cluttered and agitating
beyond itself like an atom. And so, he has set up his rod and
his line as if there has only ever been the one Experiment.

*

A man casts out, in love with the long arc of flight.
This, the wing he can soar with
and assume a kite-flier's attention to space.
But when the reel stops, he turns a sharp eye to the coast.

*

Will he be the runner in the long race
and the reel the slow, gentle runner on the spot?

*

This reel sounds angry – high heels on wood.

*

And this reel is sharp and quick and the beach
is the sound of a knitter in a lonely house.

*

At night on the shore under a moon faintly telecast
beyond the chorus of the waves
the reel is running its one thread
chattering to itself like a child.

*

In front of the lonely screen at night
he stands with the dial of the reel at his wrist
like a cracksman gentling his lock.

*

Slowly, deliberately, as if a lens
were being wound onto a slide –
the reel is ticking, exploring the depths
with a hook. And he stand ready for whatever
shall be lifted up – as if a single stitch
were to be hoisted into the dimensions of a banner
and carried forward by a people.

*

This reel is an arrow clattering its target
and the man is lost
in the sudden unthinkable music
on a dark night, the surf breaking over the rocks.

*

Preparing for thought, for the long answer,
for a chapter's pleasure –
he stands firmly on sand, he baits the hook.
The lens moves slightly in its frame.
The hook gleams, the reel ticks.

*

But what shall he cast his long attention to
when he wants the tide to be understood?
He watches the sea run loosely up the shore and knows
the reel is the worried thought he must take into his sleep.

Mud Crabs, Low Tide

I feel a sharpness under the surface like tin-tacks,
having come down to their soft mud among smells
where most would retch. They sift broken bits,
tuck into their mud; the bay has the sound

that could suck a crab claw clean: a low-tide restaurant.
Like the guileless yachts, or tunes
of light sociable chopsticks: their lilting suck and clink –
but it stops when you move, when the wind changes,

or when you ask what is their beginning or end?
Millennia ago there may have been a life for them
separate from the shore. Now they mechanically mudwallow –
half-pig, half earth-moving equipment,

before they're dragged up on lines, harnessed and killed.
Clamped together they will clang into a bucket.
They'll try to scuttle away on claws like tin openers.
But a time waits in the mangroves

when branches will basket leaves to the tide.
They accept the sun that drenches them,
the mud and its fetor, the shore and its equivocal messages,
the moon shining in the ranks of their claws.

Yachts pick (cutlery tinkering an appetite)
and they thimble quickly back, their eyes needling
like blind men's cues feeling for holes.
The tide comes and the river pours. By morning

they will have pulled themselves
through the same acres. I think of the
tinkling, the rattling in the enormous troughs
they're thrown into by the bucketful in kitchens,

steam kettling their flesh. The sun walks high
over dark mud and the made beach of their generations.
How long must they pace the brown field,
how long to endlessly dredge the sweet, the sour earth?

Eyepiece

Tonight, this place looks
like a slide being viewed
under a microscope –
the spirochetes

of dust, these ceaseless
dividing clouds.
A living biomass
moving quicker than

time-lapse, swimming
in light like
biotic fluid. All
that water's moving

as if being shifted
through magnitudes.
Flowers flicked through
focuses that sharpen

and blur. These trees
coloured like dots
of lens-thinned blood,
the air's thick

and quivering
as swamp water brought
to life.
And on the lake

the moon grows oblong
as a cell ready to divide.
The reflector tilts.
Night clouds the lens.

Japanese Cranes

Their frames –
an architecture of paper,
lightweight beams.

A low sun
huddles into fir trees, ponds –
trims the landscape.

Only the small
or poised, will survive:
these birds'

light breakable beauty.
Mating – they are
the original origami:

one unritualised peck
could chip them.
Such a skilled brittle

elegance. Earth can crack
its icy ceramic:
so their dance is brief,

a perfect choreography.
Their cries –
the rattle of tea sets

kept intact
by ceremony.
And when they lift –

they could be glass
blown from a white
clear flame.

At the End of the Day

The sun is westering. Shadows litter
the streets. Now that the heat is gone,
the air's expressionless. I search its
blank face for signs or recognition,

but the sun fading from the day
is like backing fading from the mirror.
The day lifts its touch
and my senses lose their assurance.

There is no comfort now in the city
that's pulling apart, or the people
whose eyes change like dice.
I watch the landscape withdraw and recede

leaving me to consider the silence
through which I move.
The images are gone. I become
just a breath mark across dark glass.

Situation

Now, evening's over the houses.
Who lives in them?
The street is a dark seal
my voice cannot break.

Alone, I go up into my room.
My heart's hushed and hot
as sand nothing but the sun
has crossed for centuries.

From the other houses I hear
voices, wet with laughter.
The hearts of children fizzing
in them like lumps of sherbet.

My own tongue's dumb as a foetus.
I cannot even remember
poems to set like grates
over this pit of silence.

Tonight, if dreams come they
will be small and distant.
No moon will brave the
black of the infinite.

Last Walk

for Chris

We climb down into the valley. I'm tired,
my knees are shaking: shocked. Yet I love the bush
in winter and in wind. At sunset the wind
will blow to fire all the hazel of the bush.

Now, it's midday. The creek is the sound
of pirate-red parrots crowding pockets with silver.
I see benumbed trunks, all that paper
rolled into cold, tablet-hard wood.

I could spend days powdering that bark
in my fingers like the wind. But tomorrow moves on
and will soon chill like an accurate glass.
Birds move to their trees and I think of private talk

on the edge of winter, your voice soft, hurried
by the wind; swept leaves in bush-hut hours;
parrots the sound of children sleeping out at dusk.
I imagine years from now, we will be walkers

separating from the group to tell each other
how once we camped here alone, under
just the flier of a tent, how cattle lost years back
came to the camp fire to eat and moan.

Now, I hear the creek: all that rush and trickle
through an uneven valley: the hard even breath
of a runner before a marathon: the creek
braiding its leg-muscle to the road. And I

keep wondering if we'll make it. Sometimes, I see
the wind reduce the cliff face one grain at a time.
The wind is always looking for what's lost,
turning back everything like the poor

at rummage sales. The birds make me think
of rain, of ripples slipping from a bank, the rush
of a channel through a declivity. And I hear
that same sound for miles through the trees:

a thin tapered canoe down the hard-training
and trackless slopes. I stare into the distance
with a feeling that a little more
of the rock has been carried off as dust.

On Polling Day

They come from houses, factories.
My pen's busy over the page. All day
I add and subtract as on a bursar's ledger
those who belong to the institution of Australia.

We tally under grey-white collars
like enumeration clerks who settle our taxes.
But this is polling day – voting lines
trail like meal queues across the country.

I watch the people walk in: their faces
say you can pay and pay and still own nothing.
Fences and property lines wash away like sand.
I am an official hunting out names like anthems:

citizen or non-citizen? ready to draw
a thin red line like a blood vessel through the names.
But these are migrants. And they know
you can deed poll a name of its nationality.

For how many of us is Australia just a web
walked into from the old districts, shires and provinces?
We are all floated from a different place
we don't remember but still believe in,

like our birth. An old man talks to himself,
his face shawled in his thoughts, memories of governments.
He offers me his name on a piece of paper
and a message declaring himself skilled

but of no property. I see them all come in
like blood donors. And what must I declare myself?
what colours? – just throwing green into the sea?
In my country as if on a vacant stretch of beach,

I wonder about the old, true nation
that was once a dense complex of sites
not easily transgressed; the names of its people
written in the long documents of dunes,

in old shells that stitched skin to the wind.
People who when asked their district
could say: sand, wealthiest of roads;
occupation? – walkers following the sun.

The Bee Keeper

He hunts bees, those workers that dance
for pollen. Like caravans that wander incense routes
East in his garden. They buzz as they scrub out
their cells with the salt and chastity of devotion.

Later, they'll drool honey. Yet sweetness
can turn sour and today they have collected
from the crippled plum and there is bitterness
amongst the roses, mutiny in the hepatica.

He watches them enter petals like vestries
in which to pray. But he knows piety can turn
in a treachery of light. One day, they'll compute
the sun for an exit; a choreography telling them:

left at the rock, three times round the tree.
So he listens for them in their noisy gazebos
and ponders loyalty, servitude. They were hers.
She'd hold a jar of them to the light,

small as dried camomile flowers; she kept them
amongst the cheaper daisies. A solitary man,
he remembers how, once close to his ears,
they sounded like knives in an attic of terrors.

The air leaked no scent of her betrayal. Yes,
he will rip up those plants. Now, he watches
for the queen. Is she plotting to leave
with the dance of another promised scent?

Any moment they could swarm; like Guy Fawkes
sparking the death of his own effigy.
But amongst his roses is strewn bitter gunpowder.
And now the bees like apprentices hand him

veil and gloves. They hood his fanaticism;
they dress him in the vestments of terror;
they hum him notes of a requiem; they plot
their routes; they are yellow with addiction.

He could burn them, he thinks, remembering
her lips crushed against his, bitter
as saccharine. His passion could tear
like a blowtorch through those racks of honeycomb.

White Peacock

The feathers lift –
like the sudden coming on
of sprinklered water
over imperial lawns.

Breeze-shaken and trembling –
you imagine the break
into a drift of wish flowers.

Now the fan streaming with dance –
(imagine the face of an
angel
streaming with light
in an annunciation).

It's the lovely silver rippling
at a saint's fingertips
in a Kirlian
photograph.

Seeing
is like entering a Chinese shop
full of paper lanterns –
voices whispering
in room after room like hands
caressing ceremonial silk –

until you come out
to a farmyard screeching of hens.
The peacock is just another sad rag-picker
about a cage, alone

in the knowledge of its palatial etiquette.
It goes about the pen-muck
with the geese,
the yokels of turkeys
slubbering at scraps, hen-poor.

Its chicken-wire existence
against which the tail, at times,
flounces itself
like a Marie Antoinette

or glows like
Saint Theresa among the stricken.

The Herons

Then the path wound down
to a browner place, to a river
where rain-grey herons slender as rushes
drifted off like camp smoke.

I've only seen their colour
in a few opals baked deep in clay country.
When they stared, it was as if
their eyes carried on

through emanations.
One stood so peacefully
as if it saw and heard the single
far off, crystal note;

slender, rag-thin bird we called
blue Gotama. We crumbled a mushroom –
all we could call
sacred, yet common:

but they looked past all hungers.
So we trod quietly back,
left them sitting above the long
brown earthworm of the river

and our pile of useless
vegetable soil. They were
beautiful as blue veins in the wrists of monks
fasting for perfection.

In the Park

Sitting on the grass
in the park – thinking about
what's going by, about
the pinks and plenary reds

of today's sunset.
Insects rampant as ions
off charged wires nipping,
tingling my legs.

Those buildings are like
bottles of scent fragile
in their lemon spray
mist and cologne light.

The harbour's becoming
dark against the chromocosm
of the moon adrift
under the stars.

A gull squeaks – it's
the sound of a pin
piercing polystyrene – it
carries out to the yacht masts

moving mechanically
as wiper-bars, out to
the Opera House, a cluster
of starched serviettes.

Now, out to the suburbs,
those racks and racks
of tinted light
rising behind the trees.

Walking in the Angophora Forest at Night

There is a way back out of this bush
we can only find by torchlight.
You shine a low beam on the path ahead:
a round, white foothold. The leaves rustle

like small marsupials that see us
with awakened light in their eyes.
Trees are the sudden, vivid white
of cockatoos sleeping on branches.

You raise the beam to pick up
the cool, low voice of an owl as if it
questioned the trespass of ghosts, or someone
treading as thoroughly as this light.

I don't want to go back to the road,
to the car under a streetlight.
It is good to walk in the dark
with a torch's immaculate hold.

We hear from leaf to leaf the fall
of water drops; frogs in the creek the glug
of old drains; the bush move like a bird
with abeam trained on its heart –

as if we'd opened a shutter to the
light from a cold, winter afternoon.
Our eyes like fingertips pull
a chill to them. If you shine a light

into the heart of an owl,
ghosts will respond with their names.
You walk on, switch off the torch and call.
Your voice flies through the shutter

as if it found the window for looking through –
the blue of a kingfisher in full daylight,
awake and calling. But we'll step back
into our bodies like birds

to their branches, because
in the knowledge of the afternoon
there is darkness and a call.

Streets of Chippendale

Streets named Ivy, Vine, Rose and Myrtle –
now lack a single tree. They could have been
the homes of kindly aunts in quiet suburbs
before factories like terrible relations

moved in, changed the place.
And Abercrombie (sounds like an eccentric,
unmarried third cousin) – you expect a place
where residents dressed in slacks and turtlenecks

are walking pedigree dogs;
but Abercrombie's different –
hits the bottle with a dozen pubs,
grumbles like a drunk parent

to 'bloody well watch the road' as it crosses
to Hugo, Louis – they could be
respected gentlemen strolling past terraces
to call on the nearby Aunts:

but they're beer-mates of Abercrombie,
pub-crawlers that back onto Caroline in the dark,
where someone smashes the street lights.
Sad daughter of the ruined slipper –

your body a mass of work-boot bruises.
Thomas and Edward have climbed
to renovated villas, leisure-hour balconies,
trees, incomes. Abercrombie screeches cars,

questions their manhood, lands in trouble
with the police. Streets change character.
Suburbs go to the wall like families.
Ivy, Vine, Rose and Myrtle not one of your descendants

mourns your loss. Christian names mean nothing.
Your surname's dragged through police files –
strikes fear in pedestrians
who stray into one of its dark corners.

Wind

The last of the day
is burning off in streets.
Far off, those trees churning lightly
as smoke behind
shut windows, doors.

Scrap-paper wind blows down
all the long street
broken up into
bits of rainwater –
these houses lustreless,

thin as Lebanese bread.
The day is cooling.
The air feels as if it is
filling with water;
it's only the wind.

Trees churning at the window.
Bits of the day
badly pegged along
the skyline
as washing flaps along

back fences.
The wind is the sound
of pills dissolving in trees
or a radio channel gone
off the air –

here, where it catches the high wires
it's like someone's far-off
humming in all
the pouring water
of its branches.

The Two Brothers

I just wanted to keep the snails away from those brothers.
The ones who in the back garden had shown me themselves,
grinning queerly as when they'd shown me lizards they'd killed,
or sparrows they'd slowly bled with a needle. They tucked

themselves back into their shorts, next to their pockets
where they kept their things to torment me. I collected snails
and hid them in a neglected part of the garden, though always
some flower would let them cobble and feed at its stem.

The snails never needed more than a single leaf to paint
picture books for a child, the two wands at their heads touching.
When I picked them, they'd delicately immure themselves
into their shells. But those boys, big with the world

in their pockets, would dare each other any taste, any soft clot,
any ugly act. When they made tattered lace of a snail
sprinkling it with salt, I clenched my mouth to my knuckles
and felt tears in the circle of my mouth. I knew this moment

as bitterness held to the tongue, as if next those brothers
would kiss me if I cried any louder, or told.
We watched the snails boil and froth like illicit stills.
They pushed twigs in the snails that tried to clamp

softly together, that writhed in salt like epilepsy (a brew
they dared each other, worse than the froth on swamps).
These brothers who had shown me dead birds in their pockets;
how many grains of salt it took to evict a small snail;

the fate of any spider they found squatting in the loose shells.
But when they had held themselves in their hands,
they shook a little, not quite sure what they possessed
and touched themselves through the emptiness
of their pockets, scared they'd find the prize of nothing.

Dining Out

after Gilbert Sorrentino

for Chris

Cochineals and fig colours ripple
into the bedroom. A breeze gets up
from the deckchair of a yacht.
The light's all marshmallow and angel food.
In this moment that is precise
for tasting, we watch the night come on.
You kiss me, drug my taste buds
and the room swirls like the hundred dishes
in a revolving restaurant and we're not here
we're there, at the Summit! where your eyes
rarefy into clear tea, or maybe
maple soup, or Spanish brandy
picayunes and roasted burritos
and, darling, I think I'm getting drunk.
Do enzymes work like contraceptives
I ask as my senses fall mellifluously
as brocade over the foyer
as we're about to hit the fresh air,
stepping over the possibility of tomorrow
as just so much spilt milk. And now,
under the last goose's egg of light
I crave that my heart will brace,
stay clear, unfurred,
know what you are: pure precise taste
of lemonade in the dark field of the fair.

Flower of Flowers

A smell is rising from our bodies like a dark potato. We can't get rid of it, as if our hands are grubby with digging. It is in the wood, in the lemon, in the container of oils; damp and spidery, an under-the-house smell. It is in our clothes, in the fickle breath of the wind. We bring a cellar smell into the open garden.

We rub a rind back to its pith, crush leaves on our skin hoping its soaps will lead us back to a trellis of perfumes, the lemon to its sherbets, and the earth to inodorous snow through which can leak only the scent of rare, blue poppy.

But wherever we go, on our hands is the smell of the dead unlifted to their graves, the smell of unpaid work, the kitchen smell, the smell of sinks and peelings, the cold smell of a stone turned over, the smell of moss, of drains, the smell of a stray, dark child wandering a bewildered corridor.

It is the smell of the earth raked, trodden-down, worked-over, battled-on. When we go out to the garden we feel like peasants whose bodies are the fruit of a plantation that is spoiling their whole lives.

Oh violet and mint, marjoram, palm oil, cypress, meadowsweet, sweet-cinnamon, calumus, cassia, olive oil, gingergrass, sweet flag and honey, sweet wine and almonds, tea tree, pimento, neroli and ylang-ylang which once meant flower of flowers!

Chinese Explorer in Africa: 15th Century

The jungle sucks. The air drags – a heavy, wet leech.
I long for the order of the Emperor's imperial garden –
its vines on trellises, its growth clipped back
like an insurrection. We have stared
into the jungle's cursed jade.

Under this heavy night I study my orders.
Tomorrow in Zanzibar we capture slaves and animals
for the Emperor's zoo and torture chamber.
The natives will trade ambergris and ivory,
for spices, gold and tortoise shell –

we can lead them into ships just by offering them
peacock feathers. But I cannot sleep.
A hot wind blows off a sky the colour of wet gunpowder.
I think of our own light winds
tossed in the soft shanghai of our sails,

back at the palace my Egyptian concubines
their laughter like Peking lanterns
their rich, aubergine skins. But I have been warned –
if I fail my fate will be serving the Emperor
in his fleet of Grand Eunuchs.
Now, I quote from Li Po and kiss my panda's foot.
I wish for the luck of capturing a giraffe
and on my return to be received by the Emperor
in the Grand Hall of Receptions.

Hannibal on the Alps

Tonight, it's quiet. Exhausted my men sleep
though they've learned to waken
from their best dreams. Our weapons
at least temper sleep like whores.

Below the small campfires burn out.
I can remember our farewell fires
on the plains of Utica and on the harbours
as our sails tusked the wind to Spain.

Perhaps we should have taken the sea –
the Mediterranean soft under our backs.
Here, the wind's cold and smells of wolves
I've seen rip our young elephants

like soft rind. And even now I hear
those terrified cries of my men and my battle
elephants that stumbled at the precipice.
Nights pass, but time's no champion.

Tonight, the cold sacks my sleep.
If only I could be one of my deserters
asleep under the glossy stars, or by now
drunk on the musty grape of Andalusia

clamouring for music and extravagance.
Now, I listen as the wolves
drive a goat off into the valley.
At dawn we count our losses and move south.

The Eunuch's Lament

Outside, in the courtyard of the Begging Bowl pagoda
peacocks mate. Like any upper-echelon eunuch
that terrible yin voice is tottering and high-pitched.
It is Spring, leaves blossom like the mouths

of little dragons; green shoots sproggle
out of black earth. But a season can be brutal
as any man, any rough soldier. I stare backwards.
My eyes are telescopes looking for impossible stars.

Perhaps, better to be a silkworm than wedged
between the Court and the Bureaucracy
just living for prize favour, just the same sky
cracking my thin glass of anguish. Thinner than

a monk's prayer shawl, fragile as lantern paper –
favour will not last longer than moonlight in the trees.
So who wouldn't pick off the Emperor's prize grubs
to stuff their own pockets with silk, to have

something to spin a life with? But what am I?
A boy poling himself off from one inhospitable shore
of memory to another, gauging a future
by horoscope, by season? No man drinks rice wine

through a pipette. No man picks azaleas of pleasure
where life is an orchid wasting its perfume
at the back of the Palace fountain.
What am I? A daughter with my sex unmanned?

No matter how much ginseng, my flesh won't change.
No man's heart is the gland doing it all.
Will the wind forever trail a cut voice
through the water lilies? Will the butterflies,

monarchs unto themselves, float freely in the dusk?
What am I, what forgery? When a dragonfly hovers
in the air, the wind carries the voice's undanced cadence.
You can hear eunuchs fall with a scream.

The Blue Bulb

It's evening and I'm staring into the oracular light of my room's single bulb. I'm staring until my vision becomes holed and these holes appear as if they are filling with sand.

This paper is full of sand, fine-grained sand and I am not writing words I am modelling sand into the shape of words.

Hour after hour staring into the bulb until huge amounts of sand pour from my eyes.

There's a knock at the door and X arrives clumsily tripping over the last word I've modelled in the sentence 'in the desert of silence every grain moves every other grain'. X has brought with him a blue bulb for the vision of water. At our mutual point of focus water channels into the sand. And I am no longer modelling sand into the shape of words, but modelling words into oases. Sitting in the oases of words modelling oases.

Now, we try something entirely different. X replaces the blue bulb with a black bulb for the vision of silence. I am no longer modelling sand into the shape of words, nor modelling words into oases, I'm chipping away at a very hard rock – a rock composed of the grains in the sentence I'd modelled from sand and mentioned in a previous paragraph.

I chip too hard and the bulb shatters, plunging the room into darkness. X yells stubbing his toe on the rock while looking amongst the debris for his blue bulb.

Address from the Curved City

For five years I've lived in the curved city. As I say this now, it is difficult for me to adjust to the particular geometry of your vowels, having spoken for so long nothing but the beautiful variations of the vowel 'O'. Flattening my tongue against the roof of my mouth, pushing my lips into an almost straight line is a dreadful discomfort. Think of the beautiful vowel 'O'. The only vowel whose symbol exactly articulates itself in the human body.

In the curved city, we are at peace knowing language and landscape pose no threat to each other's design. Our terraces, our cloisters, our alcoves, our libraries are no less impure in vocal than in visual form. You who live in a world whose language and architecture have a purely arbitrary relationship can have no understanding of our aesthetic. Only a language such as yours, demotic and crude, could allow the dishonesty of the statement: 'the vowel "O" is produced in the voice box.'

It is the principle of the curved city that unless a person is attuned to a place by their very breath they cannot have true peace. We have discovered our peace through the beautiful vowel 'O'. We have discovered in the curved city a propinquity with our world that you can only minutely approach through cries of pain.

So perfect is the conception of the curved city that on my arrival my legs went from point to point, not in their usual linear way, but imperceptibly via the circuitous. As if my whole body became immediately tuned in to the aesthetic. Since arriving, I have not once felt at variance nor thought of the place from which I came. Only now in speaking these words do I remember the streets, the vertical and horizontal escarpments, the houses, the corpses outstretched, the faces and the mouths contorting, the orders and the bodies massed into those unspeakable mounds.

The Dispossessed Angels

Now, we are grounded. Once we were
like windmills turning on fertile slopes.
The air made us dizzy, spun our heads like propellers.
Weathervanes lifted us off our feet.
We were the power source that saved souls!

Now, we don't even know where the water is,
or what to do with the wind, except
hoist it high in our cheeks and keep it there.
People, they say your mountains breathe
like bedridden invalids. Is it true –

will we go up to those hushed peaks?
We have heard how in the high mountains
breath is white light marbled with subtle oils.
And isn't breath something to stir the silver
alive, a wish for an angel?

In a ravine now, we sit remembering –
how we lost our foothold and plummeted.
Still our hearts uncork in our ears –
as if at some terrifying level. And we don't
breathe easily. We pant looking up
at those terrible and trackless slopes.

Blue vistas may revive us and peaks
gently resuscitate true breathing.
But we wonder by what fragile cohesion
the body keeps the soul floating
above a treacherous landscape.

Often we've watched ourselves: as if we were
tiny bubbles levitating over a hair brush.
So what do we do, trapped in the ground state
of our terror? In the soul's slipstream
maybe we'll lift a few inches.

But now we follow the flat drawl of the horizon
(though our power weakens the closer to sea level).
Oh, to look down or up and not panic.
Do you know how it is? Then imagine how it is:
our glorioles blackened by fossil fuel
when they could have been brilliant and blue.

Angel-glass

for Dorothy Porter

And up ten thousand feet
to the edge of light
to the lens-makers of angels
to the philharmonic silences of glass

where the faintest whisper will shake in each transformed
grain of sand
where the lovely sonar
of God's voice will call and call through.

A lip put to a piece of angel-glass
(an old Roman perfume bottle
to which we've lost the secret of its glaze)
will feel the incipient mantra of its shells.
Only one sound
will call the glass back
to the ocean.

In the hyacinth-pink air of the upper Universe
you can see the angels
(who do not exist for silence)
working away at a stubborn crystal
becoming lens after lens after lens

through which can be seen
stars, skylights, mirrors ever-deepening,
cascades in music,
dream-wanded nights,
days of evaporated coolness

and just one glance will
make us dizzy, our heads ringing
in the infinite
air bells of a crystal.
A shrine that's caught

the world:
like this piece from an old bottle –
dusty, but floated with light,
translucent, voice-delicate,
beautiful
as spell-glazed eyes
dawn-deep in glass.

The Clerical Angel

My voice is a dizzy altitude.
I dream all the robes
of my hair are tied up
in a pin of anniversary silver.

There are so many obese records
to flick through, to file
at a desk overlooking
the slum end of the universe.

It's too bad for an angel
clothes stiff as lampshades
on a student's budget,
only a rope quoit for my hair,

God looking shabby in his
lab coat, mixing chemicals.
I long to sing! –
but these days the organ-pipes

are test tubes and bubble without variety.
'Les Sylphides, Les Sylphides' I hum
while God shouts back to me
'NO! the sulphides, the sulphides' –

his face deadly as asbestos,
running me from beaker to beaker
frothing with esters.
I must wait out the hot bouts

of the beakers, or till heaven changes.
I'm Pianissimo, the angel,
dreaming of halos, not halogens,
of Haydn, not hydrogen,

of keytones, not ketones –
my angst is so many angstroms,
measuring milligrams for millenniums
and cursing the language.

All the chemicals in the air
have turned my hair (once
blooming golden under
the spotlights I'd sing for)

into locks gooey as mozzarella.
Oh! the days when the only
vibration that mattered was music!
The old gifts are lost.

Now an angel's voice rasps
against music like a bunsen
boiling dry a dish of pure water.
I long for the old order.

I hear the seconds of my life tick off
into gamma-ray flak like a record
spitting off at the centre
after the song has ended.

And what does an angel do
when all he wants is music?
These days even the cherubs no longer
love their Cherubini.

It's Pauli now
and the rock forms of the atom.
Planck vs Franck for the music
of the spheres.

Performing Angels

When the vestibule's all light
& stars sway like a night of sung carols –
can you hear us?

Our clear castrati voices as we bump
into the props
of old morality plays,
the seraphim cooing
for the soft focus of cathedrals.

We try all night
to get the sounds right,
God singing directions
like an overzealous catechist,
the cherubim as if squeezed through a piccolo.

Those old akashic tapes:
voice upon voice upon voice upon voice:
a choir of ages.
Sometimes you'll hear
the operatics of a requiem

through your thicker air,
here attenuated to Mozart, lighter
breakfast music. (Short of decibels
the idea of rock's exotic – but unpentecostal
as a gravelly-voiced angel.)

Hour after hour we practise
the exact timbre
of a drum roll that in our thinner atmosphere
goes soft, quiet
as time-pips.
Our place on the eternal scale
is as measurement –

note by pinnacle note
against the seismic sound of the occult,
or psyches tuned so low off the known scale
& trembling with a terrible stage fright
under the spotlights of our halos.

We sing!
just one cycle per lifetime
but our range is infinite.
Hear us penny whistle
the hour: ourselves
and the lovely Rehearsing Ages.

The Fall of Angels

a poem ending on a version of a line by Czeslaw Milosz

Our heirloom faces cracked like china plates.
It all happened that day, at practice.
We were pealing off the scales, one by one
when one of us bit into that note:
the high, high, highest E –
the god note, monarch of all notes.
One of us, tempted too much,
inched his throat and touched it.

For a single second we all listened, stunned.
Then came the aeons of glass shattering,
each note broke a million panes.
We were shivering, trembling.
Music rebelled against us like a war of forces.
The notes annihilated each other.
Cs killed Cs.
Scales undid themselves like threads
pulled out of our bodies
and tones clobbered semitones from rocky heights
until nothing breathed off a dead scale.

When it ceased, our ears stung
as if they'd been tortured with electrodes.
We stood with broken wills and cracked faces,
our voices gone. Singers had become sinners.
Now, when we open our mouths nothing comes.
It is the grief of angels to have to belch
into each other's faces for excitement.

We are imprisoned in the gulags of dead voice boxes.
The voice is subversive.
The power of the note is absolute.
But people, we do not even have the hullabaloo
of many tongues to proclaim the mortality of language.

Mirrors

I must tell you everything.
My mania for mirrors.

Always when I dream of deserts they are enormous plains
of crushed glass. Sometimes I dream I am instructed
by the Highest Orders to plant
where the long shadows of the Earth
and the long shadows of other planets
all cling together – the seed of a mirror.

If anyone should tell me that mirrors are formidable
or that mirror-gazing is destructive –
I would answer 'nonsense'.
The potential of mirrors for public good has yet
to be fully realised.

My ambition is to have the most unique collection
of mirrors in the world:
the mirror through which Leonardo disguised his handwriting,
the mirror in Matisse's *The Anemones and the Mirror*,
Miro's mirror, Dante's mirror, the secret mirror of the Pope…

If my tongue were a mirror
then I'd lick up the sun's messages.
Such is my trust in mirrors
that when my enemy invites me into his chamber
of a thousand mirrors –
I shall accept.

My Name

Someone is prowling around the borders of my name. They have been there for days. I can't see them or hear them because in the house of my name is a room of silence and a huge window of fog. But I know they are there. My name is certified in a gold frame that hangs on the room's wall. Every time they move, it shakes.

At first I didn't worry. But now they have begun rubbing their sleeve over my name's glass. They are rubbing in circles that are gradually widening. I scream that they can't do this and repeatedly show them the gold frame. They take no notice. They keep on rubbing. They rub until the fog disappears and their face becomes visible.

Now, I am afraid for my name's safety. The frame is shaking more rapidly though I have set up all conceivable defences. I have padded my name's wall with photos of myself. I have entered my name on lists. I have dispatched letters in all possible directions.

Nothing is working. They have broken through my name's door and are wandering the secret passageways as if everything's already familiar. Perhaps they are a lost relative? When I question them they glare sharply as if to say 'who do you think you are?' I run to get them the gold frame. I look for it on the wall but all that's hanging there is this person's coat, dusty and torn.

When I return I find the locks on my name's door have been changed and I can go neither in nor out. I cannot yell 'Help!'

The Workday

The faraway look in Beb's face suggests she has just entered the background I'm painting. Later, I'll put in a warm pink splosh to match the colour of her dress crumpling against her chair as she watches the picnic going on under the painted trees I'm about to recreate in very still water.

The others arrive. The painting goes on. Carol, Marie, Lou at their desks perfect as the models I must have for women resting by the boats on a very drowsy morning.

Just leave it to the workday to bring out creative tendencies that don't appear at leisure (the sistine hours of the workday where we sit not working but imagining). Now, I add a slightly De Chirico ochre to the matching background of Beb's dress myriadly cracked like the fabric of an old painting and trailing enticingly in the water.

All morning the painting goes on. Beb still sitting on her chair in the sun under the trees by the water near the boats in the office. I add a touch of green where as yet there are no trees, nor even the idea of them in water.

Just then, the boss arrives along the dark line in the background (where the dress meets the chair), making it like a spot vulnerable to weather. Beb shifts on her chair causing the boats to rock and startling the faces of Carol and Marie and Lou making them useless now as models…

I feel like a pointillist around someone who just wants to relax, the dress half finished and the picnic abandoned as we return indoors to where it's treeless, but air-conditioned – the day hanging behind glass, away off and sunny, beyond the room's sudden thunder.

The Book of Birds

It's Tuesday and I'm standing in the queue waiting to have my nature explained to me from the book of life which is called 'The Book of Birds'. 'Where the heart rubs closest to the street there is a nest of grey pigeons.' 'Where the heart touches the infinite there is one feather of a dove.'

X has just finished and whispers in my ear 'I live closest to the wound and am a bleeding-hearted pigeon. I am trying to grow feathers of a nightingale under which still beats the heart of a bleeding-hearted pigeon.'

I am now only five days away from the front. One by one people come away whispering their secrets – 'my heart just falls into the dust – where the heart just falls into the dust there is a squabble of geese.' Or, 'my heart lives in the face of rocks and on the backs of field mice – where the heart lives in the face of rocks and on the backs of field mice there is a single, penetrating eye of a hawk.'

Now, it is my turn. I sit down. I say that my heart is forever sitting on an egg that won't hatch. They hunt through 'The Book of Birds'. I suddenly feel as if my soul were being built up bit by bit from the droppings of a vulture. Any minute I expect them to say 'vulture' – or, fearing the worst and nervous lest my friends should hear me called a 'spangled grebe' or 'scaly-breasted weebill'. But a few minutes pass and they are still hunting through 'The Book of Birds.' They try the index, the cross-references, the footnotes. They scan every page. Finally, they admit that they can find no meaning for me in 'The Book of Birds'. Stunned, I grab the book and as a last resort check under 'pied drongo'. With some relief, nothing.

But I am distraught. I wonder at the meaning of this. I have to tell my friends something so I say – where the heart has no meaning there is none other than the true and perfect ornithologist (page 203 I say, to make it sound like a quote). They are adequately impressed.

On my way home, I check the book stores to see if it was the most up-to-date edition. I contact the publishers for possible errors. Finally in desperation, I send off a letter to the author, the enlightened one out of whose wisdom the book was compiled. In my best handwriting and using a quill taken from the wing of an extinct cassowary.

A few days later, a package arrives. To my bewilderment I find no page references, no explanations. Instead, enclosed is a small incubator with a note wishing me luck, obviously scratched from the claw of a Prince Albert lyrebird from our wet, sclerophyll coastal region.

Invitation

Cooking oil putters like an engine.
My kitchen is setting its course!
Islands of palms, dishes of singed coconut.
Will you kiss me when the heat steers East?
The pan dips low over soft island music
urging me on past salt and spices
to the ingredients of erotic cooking.
I'm reading the brochures of recipes
to impress with the wide map of my food.
I like the way a carob bean maps
the Caribbean (I will say) as we overlook
the harbour and Opera House (that rack
of draining dishes). I have bought wine
the colour of betel nut; all these fruits
are my map-maker's colours. We can stain
our fingers while the moon circumnavigates.
Already in the simmer of a kiss I hear gulls calling
over estuarine landscapes. I try to steer
the flavour, arrange the colours on a plate.
The kitchen is the compass sending us onwards
and it's nearly seven exactly.
Tonight, let's savour the place names of food;
let's travel through time like a panel of tasters,
we'll follow the tongue of our native guide
and discoverer; whole tablespoons to tour with.
Islands of figs, oil carefully frying
a wild banana, a breeze gently rocks
and water murmurs like a slow sentence
lifted from the phrase book.

Whoever owns the language owns the food
though once dreaming paths may have linked
our sites. We will stare into our plates,
call all fares to our table.
I light the candles, their flames
are the soft palms of stewardesses
in the heart's wild, imagined places.

www.ingramcontent.com/pod-product-compliance
Lightning Source LLC
Chambersburg PA
CBHW071024080526
44587CB00015B/2482